DYSLEXIA MY AWESOME SUPERPOWER!

Written illustrated by

Paul M. Molnar

BILLY:
Oh man, why is it so hard to remember things and focus? I always feel like my head is in the clouds.

BILLY:
Where there is a will, there is a way. That's what my teacher tells me. I have the will, but I can't focus!

Oh man! This is so frustrating! Am I not smart? Why can't I see the words right?

BILLY:
Look at this. The letters just
bundle up and don't make sense.

BILLY:
The words are jumping right off the page!

BILLY:
I wish I was like everyone else. I wish I could focus.

BILLY:
Look at that big tree. It looks like...

BILLY:
A dinosaur!

BILLY:
Wait! Who are you?

WILL:
Hi, Billy! I am Will! You made me
with your imagination!

BILLY:
I did? Wow!

WILL:
Yeah! You have a very creative mind.
It's one of your superpowers.

BILLY:
Do I have superpowers?

WILL:
Well, yes, Billy. You have Dyslexia!
That is where you get many of your
gifts from.

BILLY:
My teacher says Dyslexia means I can't
read well, and that I can only beat
it if I practice.

WILL:
Well, yes. You will struggle with reading, but practice always helps. However, Dyslexia also means that you use another part of your brain more than the average person; isn't that exciting?

BILLY:
Yes, but how?

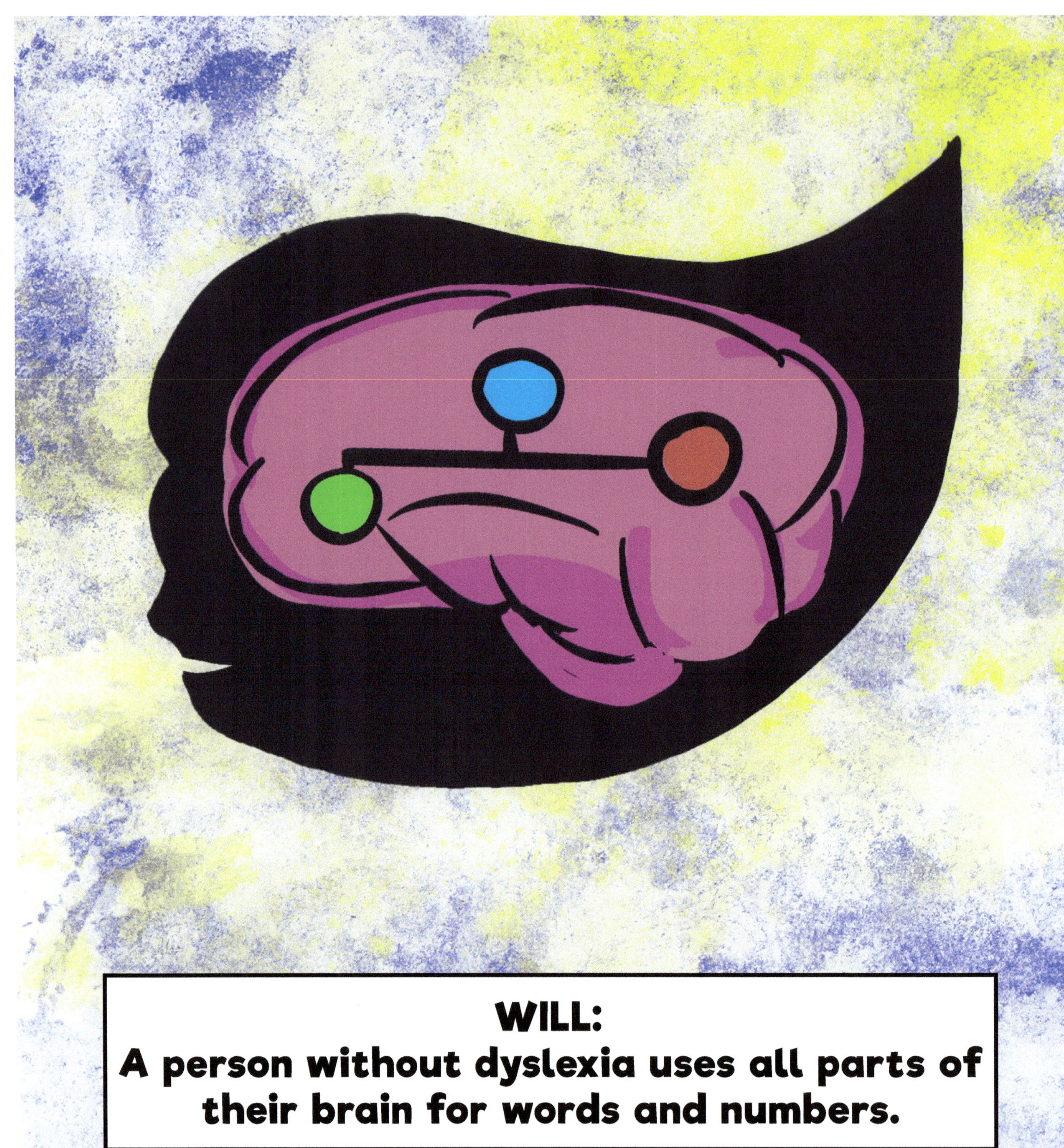

WILL:
A person without dyslexia uses all parts of
their brain for words and numbers.

WILL:
As a person with dyslexia, you use one part more
than others, an OVERactivation of Broca's area
in the FRONT of the brain!
This makes your average skills even more potent.
For example...

CREATIVITY!
WILL:
Creativity! Remember how you made that awesome robot costume for Halloween?

WILL:
You did the best costume. Painting, sculpting, drawing, building, and even creative writing are some of your strengths!

BILLY:
Writing? But those are words.

WILL:
Yes, but it takes real imagination to write well. In fact, did you know the smartest minds throughout history were dyslexic?

BILLY:
Really?

WILL:
Yes! Never forget that imagination is the preview of a future presentation.

BILLY:
Wow, that is cool, but I feel bad-especially when the teacher and my parents are trying so hard to help.

WILL:
Well, of course, you do. That's because of your EMPATHY Power!

EMPATHY!
WILL:
With your empathetic power,
You are more empathetic
than the average person.

WILL:
Meaning you are a caring person and sensitive to feelings.
WILL:
Did you know most of the greatest actors are highly empathetic?

BILLY:
Really? Wow!

WILL:
Yep, they are.
That brings me to your next super ability!

INTUITION!
WILL:
You are INTUITIVE!

BILLY:
Oh! What does that mean?

WILL:
Your perception of the world is sharper.
You have a stong gut feeling.

BILLY:
Like a space wizard from my
favorite movie, Star Battles!

WILL:
Well, from a certain point of view. Sure.

BILLY:
Okay, wow. I guess those are
pretty awesome powers.

WILL:
You are very Special. In fact, you have another power that makes you really awesome too.

WILL:
PROBLEM-SOLVING.

WILL:
Remember how you are really good at puzzles and building things? Or figuring out how to create and invent using stuff around the house? Did you know some of the world's smartest people have had dyslexia? Problem-solving comes in real handy for a genius!

WILL:
See, Billy, you're really smart. You're one of a kind! Yes, you should work on reading to grow and become a stronger reader, but always remember what you're awesome at.

WILL:
Oh, and thank you for making me with
your awesome imagination!

BILLY:
I did! Thanks to my
Dyslexia superpower!

BILLY:
I will never forget I am Awesome, and where there is a WILL, there is a way!